# On the Royal Road

Also by James Bell

*The just vanished place* (Tall-Lighthouse, London, 2008)
*fishing for beginners* (Tall-Lighthouse, London, 2010)

# On the Royal Road

## —with Hiroshige on the Tōkaidō—

### James Bell

Shearsman Books

First published in the United Kingdom in 2021 by
Shearsman Books Ltd
PO Box 4239
Swindon
SN3 9FN

Shearsman Books Ltd Registered Office
30–31 St. James Place, Mangotsfield, Bristol BS16 9JB
*(this address not for correspondence)*

www.shearsman.com

ISBN 978-1-84861-786-5

Copyright © The Estate of James Bell, 2021.

The right of James Bell to be identified as the author of this work
has been asserted by his Estate in accordance with the
Copyrights, Designs and Patents Act of 1988.
All rights reserved.

ACKNOWLEDGEMENTS
Acknowledgement is made to editors of the following publications who previously published some of these poems:
*Shearsman magazine, Journeys – A Poetry Kit eBook, Plum Tree Tavern, Long Focus Magazine.*

Several people provided valuable input into final versions of the poems here. They include:
Jim Bennett, Lesley Burt, Bob Cooper, Jan Harris, Daphne Milne,
Martha Landman and Stuart Nunn.

## Contents

Nihonbashi – Starting Point / 8
Shinagawa – 1st Station / 11
Kawasaki – 2nd Station / 12
Kanagawa – 3rd Station / 15
Hodogaya – 4th Station / 16
Totsuka – 5th Station / 19
Fujisawa – 6th Station / 20
Hiratsuka – 7th Station / 23
Ōiso – 8th Station / 24
Odawara – 9th Station / 27
Hakone – 10th Station / 28
Mishima – 11th Station / 31
Numazu – 12th Station / 32
Hara – 13th Station / 35
Yoshiwara – 14th Station / 36
Kanbara – 15th Station / 39
Yui – 16th Station / 40
Okitsu – 17th Station / 43
Ejiri – 18th Station / 44
Fuchū – 19th Station / 47
Mariko – 20th Station / 48
Okabe – 21st Station / 51
Fujieda – 22nd Station / 52
Shimada – 23rd Station / 55
Kanaya – 24th Station / 56
Nissaka – 25th Station / 59
Kakegawa – 26th Station / 60
Fukuroi – 27th Station / 63
Mitsuke – 28th Station / 64
Hamamatsu – 29th Station / 67
Maisaka – 30th Station / 68
Arai – 31st Station / 71

Shirasuka – 32nd Station  /  72
Futagawa – 33rd Station  /  75
Yoshida – 34th Station  /  76
Goyu – 35th Station  /  79
Akasaka – 36th Station  /  80
Fujikawa – 37th Station  /  83
Okazaki – 38th Station  /  84
Chiryū – 39th Station  /  87
Narumi – 40th Station  /  88
Miya – 41st Station  /  91
Kuwana – 42nd Station  /  92
Yokkaichi – 43rd Station  /  95
Ishiyakishi – 44th Station  /  98
Shōno – 45th Station  /  100
Kameyama – 46th Station  /  103
Seki – 47th Station  /  104
Sakashita – 48th Station  /  107
Tsuchiyama – 49th Station  /  108
Minakuchi – 50th Station  /  111
Ishibe – 51st Station  /  112
Kusatsu – 52nd Station  /  115
Ōtsu – 53rd Station  /  116
Sanjo-Ohashi, Kyoto – Terminus  /  119
Kyoto – Dairi  /  120

*Sample poems on Hiroshige's 53 Stations of the Tōkaidō (Great Version)*

Nihonbashi at Daybreak  /  125
The Lake Near Hakone – 10th Station  /  126
Wintry Desolation Near Hamamatsu – 29th Station  /  129
Mie River at Yokkaichi – 43rd Station  /  130
Sanjo-Ohashi, Kyoto – Terminus  /  133

Notes  /  134
Publisher's Note  /  137

The summer grasses
As if the warriors were a dream.
—*Bashō*

## Nihonbashi — Starting Point　　日本橋

after dawn no hustle and bustle
    words not heard
        a rose tinted wisp of mist

below Mount Fuji
    herds its bulk upwards once more
        unnoticed on Nihonbashi bridge

some begin their day with heavy bundles
    cross in an opposite direction
        to this daimyō's progress

all feet sound on the wooden bridge
    in soft or loud percussion
        you cannot hear them

in this vanguard of a daimyō
    only one face looks your way
        in this train of sons brothers fathers

below there are no ripples on Sumida River
    a barge and its master are in stasis –
        Hiroshige (*hard g*) has learned perspective

houses on either bank become smaller
    incrementally while moored boats
        do likewise in a cumulative V-shape

behind the centre of the bridge –
    two men lead with white plumes on poles
        that imitate black trees in the distance

all walk towards impossible futures in Kyoto
    two women who carry panniers walk into
        the present from the opposite direction

## Shinagawa — 1st Station　　品川宿

a classic three part image

first the main street of the village
  wooden houses – open fronts show tatami
    all parts of an inn

citizens – vendors – travellers walk this street
  turquoise like the sea beyond
    it all runs at an angled tilt

between Kyoto and Edo – no words –
  sea in the next part flat
    only your eyes reach for a third dimension

size is important – large boats at anchor
  two at sail reach for another world
    three skiffs squat in steps – head for shore

a spit with another village stabs the sea
  dark and light – the straight horizon
    rose and red sky announces dusk

another day in Shinagawa

## Kawasaki – 2nd Station　　川崎宿

many years before internal combustion
　　there are boats to transport ordinary people
　　　　who would fear much more than sails in the wind
　　　　　　and poles for skiffs pushed into the bottom
　　　　　　　　of this bay

where more boats surround the edges –
　　a scene interested in movement on calm water
　　　　on people who pass on the shoreline path
　　　　　　in the foreground

a stall nestled on the left among dark green trees
　　has one customer whose neck bends forward
　　　　to stare at the wares before him –
　　　　　　there's light enough to see inside

trees thrust into a sky soon to become dusk
　　slivers of mist in the distance announce nightfall
　　　　boats arrive and no others leave
　　　　　　porters still walk with bundles

horizontal lines pervade the central bay
　　illustrate back and forths while
　　　　distant lines prepare to come forward
　　　　　　as steps towards the future

soon travellers and villagers will rest
　　not knowing that the world turns all night

## Kanagawa – 3rd Station　　神奈川宿

porters carry bundles up a slope –
    you never get to see inside these burdens – tied
        they create questions in your head

they walk towards a tea house – you will
    never know if they call inside
        have just passed a more likely stall

on land most movement is right to left –
    on sea four sailing boats tend left to right
        in another language

the boats sail before high distant cliffs
    that point shard-like into the sea
        the tide is in – slivers of marsh are tentacles

seeming to reach from the sea – Akkorokamui
    come to claim its dues in the imaginations
        of those in passenger skiffs

all know it is quicker to move on water
    than on land where steepness climbs
        then lessens more slowly on foot

## Hodogaya — 4th Station 程ヶ谷宿

three trees dominate the scene where
    people appear like insects
        at this stop among the hills

the slow gestures of trees can easily
    be ignored in a busy world concerned
        with faster movement and not noticed at all

as part of this movement — partly to a stasis
    caused by the lives inside — the nutrition gained
        beside the stall that serves food has

a philosophy that hurry is unproductive
    just uses up more energy and to say
        hills roll is pure nonsense

a point of view for they stay exactly where
    they are like the trees — like the tableau
        the picture makes only its stillness

yet nobody here will hurry — pilgrims
    like trees have the same attitude inside
        their mix of concerns

both contemplate what passes
    as they stay or depart this station —
        all will go in the end

## Totsuka – 5th Station 戸塚宿

six trees lean into dusk
orange haze above distant mountains
    two porters hasten towards Totsuka
tradition says evil will happen to them
when it becomes dark
              run while others walk

the trees bend as if giant birds
about to peck the heads off travellers
    need night to do these deeds
far from the distant town
              twisted shapes of trunks
and branches suggest
        the pickings will not be good

a couple stroll into the failing light
of horizontal clouds that might
    hover forever in that day's sky
though know as we all do night will come soon
as it always does and none
           can cheat these changes

## Fujisawa — 6th Station　　藤沢宿

a place of pilgrimage to Shojokoji Temple
where you can see the arch and stone lantern
set to the left over the wooden bridge
its own slight arch soothes the way
for travellers and inevitable porters where
all walk alone intent upon their tasks
the bridge the only way to this village
of neat shops along the main street — the river
banked against flood in quiet flow beneath
you cannot tell if the river direction
is to the left or to the right though
hills in the background clothed with sea mist
suggest the river meanders towards sea
busy local people know these facts
are not interested in the same observations
are used to strangers with questions
know you will not cross back over the bridge
will visit Shojokoji and stay the night
you search for a patch of persimmons
even if the mere thought is irrational

## Hiratsuka — 7<sup>th</sup> Station     平塚宿

your eyes move first to how Mount Fuji's blank bulk
    against the sky
        emerges from the mist –
            that sense of a mighty push from below

illusion happens at a great distance –
    wind in the foreground
        rushes through trees
        and reeds to blow the sail of a boat
            on the water

travellers on poled skiffs are shards on water
    are boated to a left angle
        towards the village landing stage
two people have a horse that eats fodder –
        they will land soon

the scene will be different in an hour
    Fuji lost in a curtain of mist
        travellers and horse found lodging
the sailing boat gone and the wind eased
        a stillness about the place

## Ōiso – 8th Station     大磯宿

all horizons have infinities
    limited by straight seas
        peppered sometimes by sails

            on the edge of the world
        gradations of hills and mountains
    slip down to where dusk falls

three sails stay close to the coast
    will drop and furl soon
        beside mountains already darkened

        the village main street still bustles
    lit by lanterns from each house
as trees on shore inlets change to black

and introduce whatever sounds
    that will chime throughout the night
        before the next day dawns

        and the day's travellers still pass
    so not that time yet – paddy fields
near this day's end are still worked

26

## Odawara – 9th Station     小田原宿

the route here is a sinuous path
    four people walk upon it
        content with their separate thoughts

you can let your imagination consider
    the group of men in the background
        as they pull in unison on nets

something heavy from the sea – this
    in the opposite direction to the travellers –
        perhaps needs a collective noun to gain life

a net of fish is too easy – a net of ideas –
    a future existence that excludes tradition
        and the reliable habits of centuries

there is no sound only the sense there must be –
    so many men don't pull so hard without
        a deep animal utterance – not of comfort

to the travellers – the pilgrims – the many
    manifestations that take to this road
        contrapuntal to the heave

like the travellers we'll never see the catch
    just slip through our own lives
        like the insinuations of a fish at sea

## Hakone – 10th Station 箱根宿

most celebrated on the Tōkaidō Road
and its strange dark representation
where great blocks of stone are barely
seen on the route's escarpment

it's night where sharp hills plunge into
a sombre grey – two porters with torches
light the path for two litters with travellers inside –
you know the grey will become darker

only bare flame will light porters' flesh
the traveller's kimono – snug under canopies –
and you look down with Hiroshige
as this hard climb takes place

the angle of view increases the sense
of a darkening precipice below its silence
as if an open mouth widens
ready to swallow in one single bite

have questions you want to ask and cannot
then do ask if they will walk all night
their passengers free to sleep until dawn
or if a stopping place is close

either way the lights will go out –
an imaginary film camera on an hydraulic crane
swings round to watch the two torches fade
slowly up the path into a murky distance

## Mishima — 11ᵗʰ Station  　三島宿

first snow
imitates a part-filled page of a
                colouring book
not cold enough to freeze
       the blue of river water
one of those focal points where our
    eyes begin to see
        this first sign of life
then begin to search for others –
    the red-coated figure
        two people who wear yellow hats
who perhaps await the three travellers
        who cross a bamboo bridge
why else would anybody emerge
        in this weather
where there is no sign of a road –
Mount Fuji almost blends into
    a not quite white background
an omen
        or just a fact of life
virgin snow is a natural occurrence
    spread everywhere on
        trees and houses
and threatens in the sky before the next fall

## Numazu — 12th Station  沼津宿

you notice first the sky
    as its white phantom of cloud
        negotiates its abstracts around the blue

the sombre bulk of Mount Fuji

a line of black rocks split the aerial
    and mundane in two where solid ground
        is a third in the foreground

your eyes must traverse a wide rice paddy
    tended by a tiny man and horse –
        on land there are the ubiquitous travellers

as the Tōkaidō road continues
    and trees give shade to the local auberge

## Hara – 13th Station　　原宿

clouds weave soft wisps around
    Mount Fuji like white dragons
you wonder if this is next day
    on the Tōkaidō – another village
where not much happens – nobody tends
    the vast rice paddy – part mist-bound
yet a day when Fuji glows in sunlight
    its constant bulk a daily comfort to those
who live in the three foreground houses
    one person watches the wind go by
as others sit out of the sun under a bouquet
    of grand trees to shade themselves in
sunless contradiction – in an insect-like manner
    below Fuji – the familiar squat some
imitate as others who pass will not
    instead travel like ants on pilgrimage
to Kyoto with pack horses and absent thoughts

## Yoshiwara — 14<sup>th</sup> Station     吉原宿

less a stopping place than a different view
    of Mount Fuji its ubiquitous shape
the eternally white summit more distant
    still visible above stands of trees
some travellers border the winding route
    their near-silent feet — hiss of a shuffle —
a muffled echo around these bending forms
    notates primal music in a newer tune
pervades the air as it slips between each branch
    into distant mist — an unbroken heart
is somewhere a sharp wind chime that barely sounds
    in the still air with each burden carried as
a dormant omen — a gift demanding its destination
    that will continue until the inevitable dusk

# Kanbara – 15th Station     蒲原宿

at a bend in the road
porters carry a client in a litter
the sky much greater than this smaller movement

a quiet village among the hills
travellers patter through on bare feet
pine needles will not hurt

gable ends of the few houses
imitate Mount Fuji – its summit
thrust up white behind the gnarled trees

an expected stillness inside these shapes
slabs of green either side of the road
a clack of branches from high wind in the quiet

## Yui – 16th Station     由比宿

contradictions between the hills
and flat stretches of grey sand
in shallow water – crossed

by temporary summer bridges
the travellers all porters who carry burdens
and care about nothing else

two locals wait and watch while
the journeys continue towards a rest
at another station before nightfall

the weight of background hills broods
over this buzz of activity
while pine trees seem to wave people farewell

## Okitsu – 17th Station      興津宿

porters carry some travellers
    on their bare backs over a river
        with a swift current

though low the water can be dangerous
    while men strive to reach Okitsu –
        among rocky hills in the near distance

their rock formations dominate the river crossing
    loom like sumo or a dull audience who
        curve one into the other as if lovers

protect the village with their indomitable size
    only part-covered in greenery
        the activities of people a distraction

this will continue until a bridge
    long and strong
        spans fast running water

                *

*Google shows quiet suburban streets*
    *tidy though gone a little to seed*
        *worn metal drain covers unaffected*
            *by earthquake*
                *there is no bridge or sign of water*

# Ejiri – 18th Station     江尻宿

you immediately look to the left
      linger on the white summit of Mount Fuji –
           above three hills it floats on clouds

clear blue sky above all this – the sky is always
      above and greater – Fuji could fade inside
           and never be seen again

become a ghost or phantom of a mountain
      that might have been here sometime or another
           above the three hills lined below with rice paddy

on the plains more paddy that cools – the progress
      of porters with burdens and simple travellers
           who walk on dry and dusty feet

are oblivious to the world they travel
      there is only the road and two great trees
           to ignore instead of all other enormities

houses are silent among small groves of bamboo
      this is a place to pass through while unable
           to take possession of the sky

## Fuchū – 19th Station 府中宿

here a plain moon
gives the only clarity

its sedate light
illuminates an active scene
where everyone is out
on the main street

people arrive and depart
by the town gate

glow from lanterns
and the moon casts
long thin shadows
in a chiaroscuro
on the ground
walked through unnoticed

still – they move
in two dimensions

## Mariko – 20ᵗʰ Station　　鞠子宿

wayfarers have stopped beside
　　　and inside a teahouse
for refreshment in afternoon shade
　　　to take a short rest
a horseman has tied his horse
　　　to the trunk of a great tree
for its coolness – everything is in shade
　　　all who still walk
walk in this sombre part of road
　　　the bright side is empty
it is usual to stay undercover
　　　life always continues as the world
turns – exists in the ordinary way
　　　later people will walk on the other side too

## Okabe – 21<sup>st</sup> Station     岡部宿

some travellers follow a serpent-
                                like route
enter hills planted with numerous
                                pine trees
on the right in a turning of the road
                                a cottage
offers rest and tea

the defile of Okabe gives access to
                a halt
desired by all

those who journey cannot see the place
      sense only their wish
            to do so
                    in growing weariness

## Fujieda — 22nd Station 藤枝宿

some porters aid travellers to traverse
a tumultuous river beside
an unusable bridge of planks

they worm their way towards the village
in a clear niche
of thick forest easy to find in the gap

the crossing is intense in the swift flow
as five porters carry five travellers
where four look back from the opposite side
five wait to go
one is turned to face you
as if posed for a photograph
in a time when cameras did not exist
the impromptu pose perhaps for Hiroshige
before the crossing of lines
of sand water and gravel before the
                                            village

is reached

## Shimada – 23rd Station 島田宿

    two palanquins and the procession
        of a daimyō traverse
    a strong river current
                encumbered only
    by high sandbanks –
                in the distance a dark
    line of hills    in amongst them
        the profile of Mount Fuji
    a contradiction ignored
            its minimal reality
        too familiar to be in a third dimension
    like the shifting sand and water
        that obstructs the lord's passage
    his retainers like him carried dry above the water
        or they make near naked progress
    waist high in the river with
        standards held upright as they
    have been all the way from Edo –
        the ephemeral ones
        among the changes of water and sand

## Kanaya — 24th Station　　金谷宿

straight lines then confusion
the first a course of moving water
the second humanity restless

there are no shadows
this the middle of day
between two stretches of water

naked except for loin cloths
some porters assist important officials
to cross a turbulent river

all stand and arrange themselves
again for the sensation of land
a bank of sand through stable

hills and forest beyond their activity
promise shelter and a solid base
only a small bridge to cross

pin figures further on walk steadily
on an unseen road that must be there
unless it is purely imaginary

## Nissaka – 25<sup>th</sup> Station    日坂宿

ten porters descend a steep slope
haul five bundles between them
into wooded hills while a colleague

climbs alone in the opposite direction
two bundles on a pole over one shoulder –
to the right four wooden houses are

a geometric border to the route – their
precise stillness echoes the shapes
carried downwards with labour and sweat

the woods appear to look upon the scene
creep over the hills as dark green wraiths
there only to attend – not to make a comment –

their silence important to what
secrets the hills have always held –
all porters – yellow badges of their trade –

understand this though nothing is ever
stated for no breath can be wasted on
what you are never supposed to know

## Kakegawa — 26th Station     掛川宿

across a wooden bridge
      near a temple surrounded by trees
a torii
      and two stone lanterns –

in the distance some hills divorced
      from the crescent of the bridge
turfed
      and cindered for extra strength

on this well-trodden way where its direction
      points towards Kyoto still far away –
for those
      who travel there on pilgrimage

will return this way and cross again
      no longer see the arc the bridge seems to make and
how perspective
      draws it to a point – an illusion of showing the way

at a period where only way-markers existed
      only the bigger picture that transcends place
distance travelled
      measured by dawn and dusk

the way life is still marked out with heart-
      beats in between – below flows
a river
      with sound that travels in another

direction contrary to the route the landward
      one takes – one that rivers always take

to reach
the sea with no stops on the journey

no stopping place if tired and wearied
      by its own flow – cinder paths ease the road
round
      obstacles to permit regular footfall

as they step into the daily rhythm's
      basic beat for finer music poetry and song
through
      this station of the Tōkaidō

# Fukuroi — 27th Station 袋井宿

everyday life is as easy as it's hard
as
    coming from the village on
                                  a road
planted with cedars that traverses
paddy fields
                a merchant leads two
loaded packhorses
                        he reaches
a farmhouse
              where
a woman lays out grains of rice to dry
on tatami
            while
                  another
carries a baby in a pouch on her back
and leads an infant by the hand
                            who
looks with the gaze of a child
on passers-by
                the conjunction
of several lives
                that meet and walk
in opposite directions
                    while
                          one stays

# Mitsuke — 28th Station  　　見附宿

in the bottom right hand corner are roofs
of two thatched houses
　　　　look accidental
as if they have crept into a photograph by error
　　　　　　　　of course this is not so
as such images do not yet exist

above on a bank two cedars
　　　　mean a pattern
　　　　　　　　begins to emerge

a rider passes on a path beside the houses
　　　　heads towards a wide river
　　　　　　　　interspersed with two banks of sand
　　　　　　　　like the roofs
and where travellers get ready to cross
in two boats at the shore
　　　　　　　　their bows pointed
　　　　　　　　　　　　like the sandbanks

and the horse drops its head
　　　　under the weight of the rider
　　　　　　　　and heavy panniers it carries
the whole makes a triangular shape
　　　　that is like a gable end

in a quiet scene where nothing much
happens

# Hamamatsu — 29th Station     浜松宿

on the right high towers of
Hamamatsu Castle
                 its fortifications
constructed with enormous blocks
     of white dressed stone
        in the middle of a forest

bordering the route at the foot
of the castle
          village houses
with a constant movement of travellers
    two riders
              one sedan chair
an ambulant merchant among others who walk

in the sky birds take off
as distant shadows
              higher-born travellers
    who mirror slower humanity
much further below
                might meet at some later point
    as both groups take the same direction

## Maisaka – 30th Station　　舞阪宿

in front of a range of sombre mountains
two large junks low in the water

advance on wind-inflated sails
towards a ragged and wooded coast

Maisaka is shelter for these vessels
sailing boats that cope with large tonnage

here stone and water can only be
traversed when you're sure of your element

where winds guide sails into rounded shapes
while cargo and passengers are still inside

pensive under canvas enclosures as
only people of the land can be at sea

need mariners to hold a sail rope – steer
above the deep below the heavens

# Arai – 31st Station　　新居宿

on the left of the quay
an inn
before which is displayed the poled signs
      of a daimyō
             who has stopped here

two or three pines and a stone lantern
      signal the importance
           of this place

a group of travellers descend from
                a boat
that has come alongside
            the dock

in the distance some sails rise or fade
      on the lake
           in reach of a far shore
beneath hills that undulate in silhouette

an idyll only in its stillness
      that pretends movement

in sky
      water
          land

## Shirasuka — 32nd Station 白須賀宿

the whole world seems to journey away
                                    from here
this thin-thatched hut
                      the only
    stillness
            in the shelter of old pines
distant ships
            in full sail
drop over the horizon

some travellers rest before they tackle
a steep
       section of the road
                       where
others have already reached the top
disappear
       one by one
              over the horizon

## Futagawa — 33ʳᵈ Station 二川宿

under an abrupt rainstorm
some travellers
                protected a little
  by capes or hats of straw or both
run towards an artisan's thatched hut
            at the foot of a wooded hill
in this area of rice paddy

Futagawa as a halt
              is fortunate
with its hut
        as
            quick feet and rain
are the only sure animation

## Yoshida — 34th Station    吉田宿

on the right a forest of pines group together
seem to lift
            the towers of an imposing castle
                  higher

a rider and some travellers cross a bridge
in the direction
            of a village
                      situated
on the other side of the river
            where boats are moored
another one prepares
            to come alongside

to join up with other boats
            in a thin link
between one side and another
where the river flows by its opposite bank
where people can cross over

the bridge in one direction or another
where the bridge is just a road
where the castle could be a mountain
that those who cross ignore

as their weariness overwhelms

## Goyu – 35th Station 御油宿

a small bridge crosses a smaller river
    in its flow towards
        the Eastern Sea
   where the horizon at that point
is pulled into the sky

   the crossing of six porters
      looks hurried
   carrying the insignia of a daimyō
through this station to the next one or
      even the one after

could make Kyoto
        in another three days
an express carrying three bundles
    so people must get out of the way
      horseback perhaps quicker

orientated in their task they run by
     trees and houses
   steps on the bridge a brief rattle

## Akasaka — 36th Station  赤坂宿

in the night
when the moon is high in the sky
a traveller leads his horse by its bridle

goes from the village on a path
that mounts into wooded hills
with an ambience of mystery

moonlight where anything could happen
though nothing moves except this traveller
and his horse and those others who walk

back to the village to be safe inside its stone walls
with spiked tops – nobody ever leaves the path –
the traveller and horse will draw further apart

from those who return to apparent safety
while trees off to the right grow darker

## Fujikawa — 37th Station 藤川宿

snow has already covered trees
and roofs of the village
continues to fall in large flakes
slows the way of a horseman
and his guide

lines of houses beside each other
pencil in the route ahead
two figures and horse the only colour
against a white world
and a dark wash for the sky
our eyes drawn towards them
as they walk away from us

trees bend in from either side
and mark their gradual passage
as do the snows of winter

## Okazaki – 38th Station     岡崎宿

from right to left a grand bridge in wood
crosses the river under which move
some skiffs – a horseman and porters
cross
        while in the distance
the towers of a castle rise at the foot
of some hills a long way off
on the bridge – high on thick stanchions
and strengthened cross beams
the procession of a daimyō
makes slow progress

maybe one met before on the Tōkaidō
that will continue forever
or until the colour fades and its paper
crumbles into dust
the deeper blue of the river
will be last – the procession of the daimyō
long gone and long dead
the bamboo of the riverbank
fully grown over and the flow of water
        entirely choked
                like there's no bamboo
                        tomorrow

## Chiryū – 39th Station　池鯉鮒宿

In front of the houses of Chiryū village
protected by a forest of bamboo
some of the inhabitants bow
for the passage of a daimyō
maybe the one who crossed the bridge at Okazaki –
some servants loaded down with boxes
while others gently lead horses from the right
as if they walk onto a stage to perform –
here to celebrate the horse fair
that attracts many merchants
and other participants – so there he walks
complete focus of attention – the main attraction
for the year after which everything returns
to how life is lived on other days –
waymarkers continue to give directions
to places nobody in the village will ever go

## Narumi – 40th Station　　鳴海宿

although dusk begins to fall
the shutters of kimono stores
are not yet closed

a merchant looks out on the street
as if in expectation of at least
one last client

one last bolt of silk or a yukata sold
though all that pass are Chōnin –
the poor in straw hats

weighed down by the burdens they carry
pilgrims with poles who ply their route –
a couple talk of the now long-gone

as is the shogunate that ruled they must
dress in plain colours – so these patterned
materials are always ignored – people

emerge from or disappear behind the hill
on the right though stilled here
in the crux of dusk and darkness

# Miya — 41ˢᵗ Station 宮宿

on the port quay to the right a grand torii
stands
    as some travellers
                    loaded down
embark and disembark
                all pass
as strangers
        concerned with themselves
with the journey each takes
                only share
this walk from here to there before
a division and individuals go somewhere else

on the left a castle rises straight from
deep water
      its ramparts impassive
both castle and torii
              are signals to boats
      out on the high sea
vague shapes that sail from here to there
and back again
        in proximity to the port

## Kuwana — 42nd Station　　桑名宿

Hiroshige did this often
showed a street scene with shops
a *mise en scène* displayed at an impossible angle
with people going about their business

the diagonal view allows interiors
to be seen better and shows these
are homes as well as shops selling products
under draped signs above wide-open doors

it is an aerial view downwards
like a movie camera on a hydraulic boom
the steepest angle bottom right
where some men stand beneath roof tiles

the trivialities they discuss now long gone
with the roof tiles and the shops – cooked food
like hot rice or noodles or miso soup
image and time cannot conjure aromas

linger perhaps on relaxed smiles
before recommencing the journey beyond here
food always the fuel for the human engine
the limbs that carry its fears and fortunes

secret philosophies inside the strictures of a daimyō
where nobody runs in town as a measure of respect –
some might think you flee from responsibilities
a reason to travel mostly with others

## Yokkaichi – 43rd Station 　　四日市宿

(i)

three boys
     impatient to see a performance
with a mask      that has a big nose
    run after a strolling player
          who ignores them
pushes his pole at the ground
      to carry him over the arch of the bridge
turfed and cindered for ease of progress
        to the village with cherry trees
in blossom behind the roofs of houses

the player bent by his effort
      mask attached to his backpack
a face he does not find funny any more

(ii)

   the wood that supports the bridge
                                          stout oak
lifts its surface like a stage
                          those who cross brief players
      like the three people who walk here
                                      for pleasure
descend from the bridge
                       about to pass the strolling player
and give no greeting to him in silent passing
                 then four pilgrims ascend from
                                  the other side
to the top of the arch
              in single file
                            intent on their pilgrimage
as if bridge and water and other people do not exist

(iii)

    the bridge is well made and lovingly kept by locals
                              expected by the shogunate
    who might travel this way too
                    create a different cast of characters
    in another short drama
                        that changes by the hour
    and the day
           and the days after
    until the bridge and its oak timbers
                            must be replaced
    or the water below no longer flows

## Ishiyakushi – 44th Station　石薬師宿

you see human chaos
travellers have stopped and rest
        from their journey
                      are disordered
though peaceful
            most semi-naked
                      wash and preen

horses drink much-wanted water
have not stopped from travel until now
shoes are changed
                loads in disarray
look discarded

a traveller who goes by sedan-chair still sits there
while his two carriers
                renew
their permits for the road with a functionary

he and four others are kept busy
inscribe order
            for porters concerned with
organising themselves for the journey ahead
       live only in the moment
              the wider landscape beyond
as indistinct as the future

## Shōno — 45th Station　　庄野宿

four porters carry a man in a litter
they run to the left
while two messengers run off to the right

their haste is in order to escape
a storm announced
by black clouds that slowly descend behind

peasants in the rice paddy nearby
who continue to work
not distracted from their task

life goes on in spite of rain
in spite of a sudden fading of the sun
all know it will return again

right at the back of their minds
they know
        the sun will return
                tomorrow

## Kameyama – 46th Station     亀山宿

travellers walk laboriously
      tired from the road that leads
         them between pines

border the entrance to the village
      under a flat castle profile against
         a grey mountain in the distance

they wear hats and capes due to chill air
      move among pleasant surroundings
         that are not a walk in the park

climb an incline on leaden bodies
      through a wooden gate that will close
         as dusk approaches

heads do not lift as weariness
      is their only guide forward –
         take to the road again
                  tomorrow

## Seki – 47th Station 関宿

it looks as if people have all lost something
and bow to find it – stare at short grass
on bended knees except for two who stand

in reality bowing to a daimyō not yet visible
a wide stretch of empty ground is cleared
to indicate his distinction – coats of arms

on cloth wave in the breeze – hang from
the canopy of a tea-house empty inside
as his procession still lumbers slowly by

down a street to the left – important officials
wait alongside trunks of possessions held
by porters beside two others who hold banners

it is a calm day with much ceremony
already present and with much more to come
a day that will end like all others

## Sakashita — 48th Station　坂下宿

at the edge of a cliff
five travellers stop near pines
to admire the void beyond
the course of a deep torrent
below hills in the distance

Kiyotaki Kannon waterfall
is celebrated by viewers
who all know the legend
of painter Kanō Motonabu who
desperate to create perfect images
to rival the real beauty of the cascade
threw his brushes in the water
in frustration

one traveller points at the fall
in amazement as he speaks
with two others while more continuing
their journey having seen this wonder
are sated by the sight

## Tsuchiyama — 49th Station　土山宿

a violent rainstorm beats down
on four travellers who hasten

along their path in a defile
between the hills — the roofs

of the village can be glimpsed
further down — in the distance

profiles of summits — blue
mountains that spare the houses

from the storm soon to abate
the mountains change to a brighter shade

## Minakuchi – 50th Station     水口宿

the name of each door is marked
by a calligraphic sign

whether they like it or not
the last travellers are trapped by the night

now the gates are closed
the only light is from the houses

the locals carry lanterns
that illuminate this scene more intensely

along with glow from house fronts
strangers caught in this street of pleasure

startled in this spotlit scene forever
and in Minakuchi until dawn

## Ishibe – 51ˢᵗ Station 石部宿

we see the interior of a tea-house
before which peonies and a plum tree
are in flower – a sure presence of spring

through open shoji we catch sight
of different rooms of the house all laid
                          with tatami

on the right a man receives a neck
and head massage from a blind person
while two women prepare some tea
                          as ceremony

in another room on the left two men
take a bath in the onsen where one soaks
                          the other dries

depicted under a large thatched roof –
all their world appears alive and relaxed

# Kusatsu – 52nd Station　草津宿

in the village
    on one side of the street
stalls offer
   tea
    raw fish
bento boxes of many kinds
     for weary travellers

some
  drink water on arrival
others prepare to take to the road again

yet another ties the reins of his tired
horse to a post –
    become still
      it already eats

we look down on this busy street scene
where the bottom left-hand corner
is silent
   see only two partial thatched ridges
      of houses
peonies again
    below in the street
in quiet contrast to such bustle

# Ōtsu – 53ʳᵈ Station     大津宿

three boats with full sails outside this bay
of Lake Biwa
            look small
                      will disappear among
                                higher hills soon
these grey to sight at the same distance

three skiffs tiny in this wide water
ferry people
            from one side
            to the other

three boats moored at the quay
at rest with
            bare masts    wait
            for pin-figure travellers
            to embark

make the whole quayside busy
ant-like with burdens and bundles
many sunhats cover heads from
            clear sky glare

a relentless washed-out orange
that whitens the lake so central
            to human activity

whose houses expand far to the left
lake water and distant hills and sky
            are untouched

## Sanjō Ōhashi, Kyoto – Terminus     三条大橋

the great Sanjō bridge terminates
      the Tōkaidō road
goes like an arrow towards
      The Imperial City
then notice the roofs of smaller houses
      on the other side of Kama River
below the mountains and hills
      that protect the city edges

the bridge is a bulge at this angle
      see no arches or building complexities
though its open wood sides
      reveal clues for us to follow
all who pass over are on foot – some in silk gowns
      that float and flow quietly in a breeze
garments that also define river direction –
      dignitaries and humble workers walk here

where some prefer the centre as their path
      will always walk this way
while some will stop and gaze upriver
      all walk and gaze in silence
I look and think I see the Kabuki theatre
      over on the right-hand side – still there
much later when the bridge is ferro-concrete
      noise too from internal combustion engines

## Kyoto – Dairi 内裏

the imposing Imperial Palace
is protected by its walls
an immense wooden gate
closed and towards which moves
a train of nobles and their servants
followed by ladies of the court –
this escort precedes a palanquin
its profile emerges from the left
of the composition – will proceed
to the right side and disappear
all having ignored the grandeur
of the palace walls – the wide
space they cross become empty
until we appear many years later
and record the scene on my
Minolta camera on Fujicolor film
in 1998 with only the two small
figures of my companions who
walk far in front as I try to photograph
the true immensity on a wide-angle lens
full-size the imposing Imperial Palace

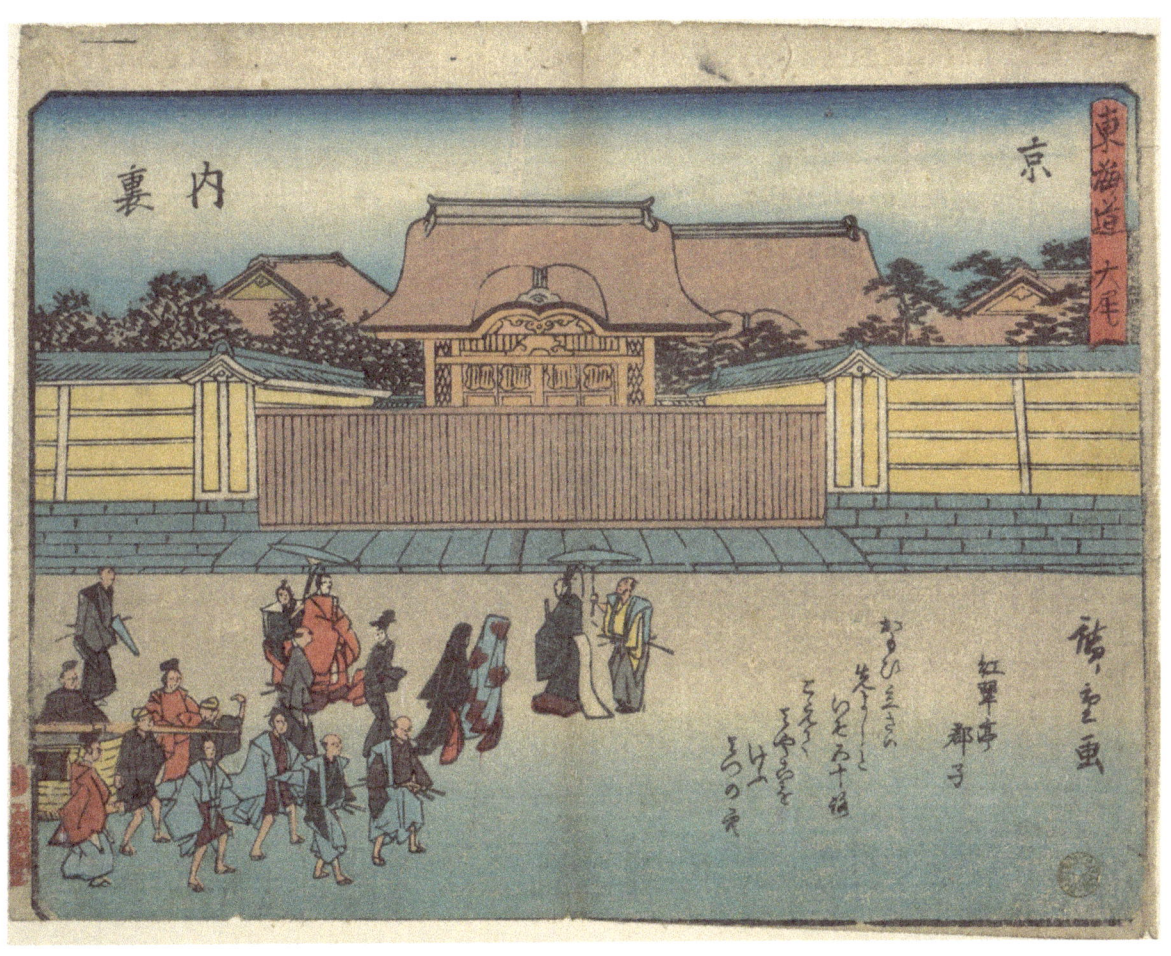

Sample Poems on Hiroshige's
53 *Stations of the Tōkaidō*
(Great Version)

## Nihonbashi at Daybreak　　日本橋　朝之景

the gate has just been opened
for none cross at night – two porters
bowed as if in obeisance

nearly reach this side *en route*
between Edo and Kyoto –
bend under the loads on their backs

ahead of the procession of their daimyō lord –
mounted
while these men are pedestrian nothings who might fall

just ahead of standard bearers
and lackeys in round straw hats – all ignored
by fishmongers returned from market

this is what happens
day in day out
as one parade or another enters and exits

there is hope in dawn sky –
two dogs sniff each other's backsides
the procession crosses

never reaches the other side
it must
on its way to or from the Shōgun

wooden bridges like this
are ornamental now for carp to swim under
and crossed daily by those who carry Nikon cameras like burdens

## The Lake Near Hakone — 10th Station 　　箱根 湖水図

      here Mount Fuji appears
over on the left as a ghostly form
      faint against the sky
easy to believe for the superstitious
as a portent    above and beyond the range
of hills and mountains of dulled colours
in blue-brown and grey    border the lake
distanced from the mountain that faces us
      its bulk makes us look there first
all else diminished    even the closer
mountain range to the right in sharper starkness
this mountain in greens and yellows –
of browns and blues and lesser grey bends
to the left in a crude nod to the lake below –
      two people in round sun-hats are almost
an afterthought    move one before the other
on a narrow path at the mountain's base
      frail and unable to influence otherwise
the enormity they negotiate on rough
laid paving to aid their way    nearly
unseen    could even be devils or sprites
uncontained in these twists and turns
      though their story and business is usually
more banal even if they choose to call
a walk through the mountains at such height
by day a once-in-a-lifetime adventure

## Wintry Desolation Near Hamamatsu — 29<sup>th</sup> Station 浜松、冬枯れの図

peasants warm themselves by
                     a fire in a grey-blue morning
one man has pulled up his clothes to warm
                     his backside
others crouch around as smoke billows
     straight up
            a white imitation of the cedar
               all shelter beside
     each composed in individual dawn rituals

the plain of snow as background
                         with stick-like trees
    dotted around
give a sketched in view of the castle
    on the horizon
       depicted schematically
with softened contours on account of distance

in the conjunction of backside and castle
we bear secret witness
to all that is concealed in what is unconcealed

## Mie River at Yokkaichi – 43rd Station    四日市　三重川

there is no focus in a whirlwind –

a solitary willow has the pragmatic curves
            that shape its nature even
      on a calm day
and now wriggles its branches into a
                      temporary confusion
      while the reeds below it shuffle in extremes
           of easy persuasion

the bare masts of boats offer straight lines
            into a non-committal sky –
      the good sense of fishermen
unseen in their houses that crouch
           in a safe covey
                    beside the masts
      beyond the reeds – keep close to a corner that
           has seen chaos reign before
                      then pass
one man's hat is blown away    he pursues heavily laden
another in a billowing cloak    goes his own way in the opposite direction

## Sanjō Ōhashi, Kyoto　　三条大橋

a bridge to somewhere from somewhere else
built for ease
    of crossing
        the Kamo
under protection of Mount Hiei
amidst the Higashiyama mountains

bridges fall eventually if wood or stone
  only dry sand cracks here under timber for now
    all can cross and do

mist drifts down the Kamo enclose houses
at the bankside
     their forms blend
into distant trees
    distant hillsides

static as the stream of people who pass
  the daimyō escort
    porters who carry bundles
  geisha with maids
    merchants ever on business
one person leans over to watch shallow water –
all gone now like the bridge
     though the mountains remain

## Notes on the Tōkaidō

In the summer of 1832 Utagawa Hiroshige is said to have joined an official delegation of the shogunate on its journey to Kyoto. This was the occasion of the annual handover of a tribute of horses to the Emperor by the Shōgun. The former, at that time, was merely a figurehead.

At the time of Hiroshige's birth in 1797, Japan was well into what became a 250-year-long closed society and at his death in 1858 was only just beginning to emerge. The origin of what caused Japan to remain a feudal society for this time period goes back to the beginning of the 17th century. Historians place the exact time as the Battle of Tennōji near Osaka Castle in the summer of 1615. An attempt had been made by warring factions to agree to "no more wars in Japan" in 1600. This agreement had been broken and was to be broken again in later years of the same century. What emerged from this battle was the first Shōgun, Ieyasu Tokugawa, who became effectively what we would now call a dictator, and his Shōgunate would be mostly hereditary until the 1860s.

As an effect of his suzerainty Japan became very inward-looking. Initially weapons, swords etc, were taken away from common people; lords (*daimyō*) had to remain in their own domains unless on the obligatory twice-yearly visit to the Shōgun in Edo, where their family members were kept hostage. The main route was the Tōkaidō Road with stopping places along the way called stations, which included eating places, tea-houses and accommodation.

Ann Wehmeyer has described these places as "new towns (that) emerged to meet the needs of traffic passing through each station, and over time, these post-station towns developed an aura of what has been described as separateness and ephemerality, becoming zones of the extraordinary and the unpredictable." Such towns have also been characterised as *sakariba,* sites filled with crowds and excitement in which the culture of *asobi* (play) arose in the context of commoner culture, apart from the official centres of power in the urban areas.

Wehmeyer goes on to talk of Hiroshige's inspiration for what turned out to be, over his lifetime, a total of 13 series on the Tōkaidō Road: "In 1832, Hiroshige had journeyed the highway as part of a firemen's brigade escorting horses to be presented to the emperor in Kyoto as a gift from the Shōgun in Edo, and it is thought that the series was inspired by this journey and the sketches he made along the way." Hiroshige was not the only artist who had seen an opportunity for doing albums of the Tōkaidō; he just did it better.

The original, which many consider the best, was issued by the publisher Hōeido in 1833–34. The second series, as presented in this volume, appeared in 1840–42 and was published by Sanoya Kihei in the same horizontal chūban format as the first series. The main difference was that this series contained a comic poem in each image, called *kyōka,* giving the name it is known by now. It is not known whether Hiroshige made yet another journey on the Tōkaidō or not, but it seems likely, as he became a successful professional artist after the publication of the first series. The second series has a quieter palette and does not display the same use of Prussian Blue as did the first. It has a sense of being improvised and figures in landscapes sometimes look like pin-figures and sketched in very quickly. He does seem to have worked quickly on some of the images and takes different viewpoints to the earlier series. He also seems to have used the series to experiment with perspective in a stylized way.

My own relationship with Hiroshige and the Tōkaidō began in 1998 with a visit to Japan. On that visit we bought a deck of cards in one of the busy city department stores in Kyoto. The cards bore interesting pictures, based on old woodblock prints, and I thought nothing more of it at the time. It was, of course, Hiroshige's first Tōkaidō, the images having appeared on all manner of consumer goods for many years. Then I bought an art book on Hiroshige, and still later started writing ekphrastic poems based on some of the images.

Later still, after moving to Brittany, in France, we visited the Hélène and Édouard Leclerc Foundation art gallery created by the founders of the French supermarket chain Leclerc, in Landerneau, Finistère. It was primarily to visit a Henry Moore exhibition, thousands of miles from Japan and its art. The shop was interesting, with the usual postcards and posters. It was there I first met and bought a copy of *Le Petit Tōkaidō* with Hiroshige's name on it and only later became more familiar with its place in the canon. The rest, as they say, is history.

SOME EXPLANATIONS:

KANAGAWA – 3ʳᴅ STATION
The Akkorokamui is a gigantic octopus-like monster from Ainu folklore, equivalent to the Nordic Kraken, which supposedly lurks in Uchiura Bay in Hokkaido. It is said that its enormous body can reach sizes of up to 33 metres in length. (Wikipedia). Hokkaido is one of the most northerly Japanese islands and the Ainu are ethnically different from other Japanese. This, and the monster, are far away from the Tōkaidō Road, bordering the Eastern Sea. This could be anachronistic. Probably residents of Kanagawa had never heard of the Akkorokamui, but I wanted a monster.

SAKASHITA – 48ᵀᴴ STATION
Kayo Motonabu (1476–1559) was a painter who, long before Hiroshige, painted the famous waterfall, Kiyotaki Kannon waterfall; in fact he did a whole series of waterfall paintings collectively called *Tour of Waterfalls in Various Provinces*. It is apparently just a legend that he threw his brushes into the falls. He was also a very pushy businessman and made a hard-sell of his own work, which suggests there is some truth in what is said and what people's opinion of him may have been.

KYOTO DAIRI – FINAL IMAGE
Unusually in this series, Hiroshige offers two images for Kyoto, the journey's destination, and the second contains the additional word *Dairi*. This is the inner palace of Daidairi, the former Japanese imperial castle in Kyoto between 1794–1868. It housed the throne chamber, the emperor's quarters, as well as those of the consort's family. It burned down in 1868, and therefore I'm being disingenuous when I claim to have photographed the same building in 1998, although it *has* been lovingly recreated.

JAMES BELL

*A note on numbering*
Some places record the Tōkaidō images with slightly different numbers, starting from Nihonbashi as Nº 1. In this book, we have followed the Japanese style – which is more logical – whereby Nihonbashi (the starting point) and Kyoto (the destination) do not have numbers: the numbers apply only to the stations along the route, where travellers stay and rest, not the beginning- and end-points.

One other small point: *Nihonbashi* is often translated as "Nihonbashi Bridge", but *bashi* actually means "bridge" and thus, in all but one case in this book, it is simply referred to as Nihonbashi. Including the word "Bridge" in English is rather like saying *Pont Neuf Bridge*, in respect of the famous location in Paris.

## Publisher's Note

James Bell sent me this manuscript in April 2021 in the hope that it would be published by Shearsman Books. Some of the poems had already appeared in *Shearsman* magazine, under my editorship, and it was thus a reasonable hope that we'd take it on. James and I had known one another for some years, and had co-hosted a poetry reading series, Uncut Poets, in Exeter for five years or so, until James retired and moved home from Devon to Brittany. Inevitably, the manuscript joined the ranks of "possibles" awaiting a clear decision; then I heard to my considerable shock that James had passed away just a month after sending me the manuscript. I chewed it over a little longer and realised that it might be possible to put together a volume that also contained all of the woodblock prints from Hiroshige's second Tōkaidō series. By odd chance, for some 35 years I've had an edition of these very same prints in miniature book form (*Down the Emperor's Road with Hiroshige*, edited by Reiko Chiba (Tokyo and Rutland, VT: Charles E. Tuttle & Co., 1965), and have often perused its pages. Once I started looking in earnest, it transpired that there was a splendid website (https://www.hiroshige.org.uk) containing all of the prints in this series, with good enough resolution for printing at the size I needed, and I downloaded all of those, straightening them up where necessary, but otherwise not interfering with the brightness, blemishes or colour. For real fans of the artist, this site also offers a synoptic view of all the artist's Tōkaidō prints by which one can see, for instance, all the Nihonbashi images on one screen. For those who prefer to concentrate on each integral series, one can also see all 50-plus images from each series on one page, and click on each image for full-screen sizes. While I could also have used this site for the five images in the Appendix, I opted instead to use images available, gratis, from Wikimedia Commons and from New York's Metropolitan Museum of Art, all of which were of good quality. Details are:

    Nihonbashi (1833/34), Wikimedia Commons.
    The Lake Near Hakone (1833/34), Wikimedia Commons.
    Hamamatsu (1833/34), Wikimedia Commons.
    Mie River, Yokkaichi (1833/34), Wikimedia Commons.
    Sanjō Ohashi (1833/34), Metropolitan Museum of Art, New York.
        (Rogers Fund, 1918, Accession Number: JP525).

Tony Frazer,
July 2021

www.ingramcontent.com/pod-product-compliance
Lightning Source LLC
Chambersburg PA
CBHW060943170426
43197CB00023B/2972